Charlie

For Jane

In a sky of blue above a sea of green,
lived a playful, young cloud named Charlie.
More than anything, Charlie wanted everyone
to notice what a special cloud he was.

He'd roll himself into a rocket ship
and soar up as high as he could go.

He'd ruffle his edges
and spiral down like a snowflake.

4

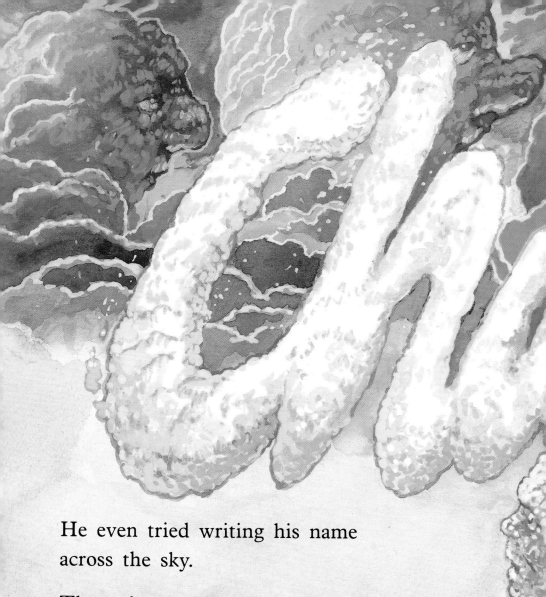

He even tried writing his name
across the sky.

The only trouble was
no one noticed.
The clouds would simply shake their heads
and float on by.

6

Disappointed,
Charlie drifted over the village.
From up high,
he could see children playing
and animals grazing in the fields.
"I know how I can get
their attention," Charlie grinned.

8

9

Extending a long, bumpy tail
and sprouting a knobbly neck,
Charlie became a dragon
charging across the sky.

Still no one paid any attention.

10

11

On kite flying day,
Charlie placed himself
right in the middle
of all the kites.

But still nobody noticed him.

In fact, no matter
what fantastic impressions he did,
no matter what great tricks
he performed, no one *ever* noticed Charlie.

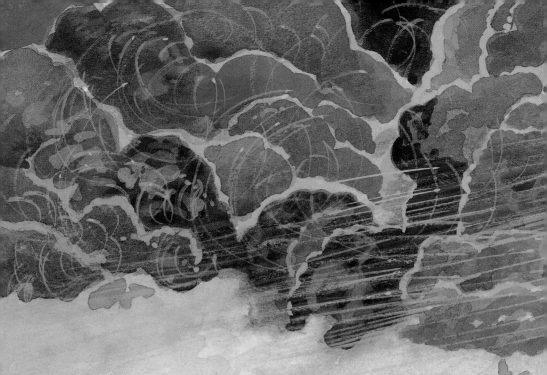

Charlie let the trade winds carry him
far out to sea.
"I guess I'm not so special after all,"
he sighed.

Drifting down,
Charlie took a long, cool drink
from the sea.
As he drank, he began to get bigger.
"Wow!" cried Charlie.
"I'm going to grow as big as I can.
Then everybody will notice me."

15

Charlie kept drinking
until he stretched to the horizon
and billowed up over the mountaintops.

When the people in the village
saw the enormous cloud,
they ran into their houses,
shut the windows,
and locked the doors.
The animals were so frightened,
they huddled under the trees.
Even the birds flew away.

Charlie tried to shout,
"Don't run away. It's me, Charlie."
But his voice sounded
like the rumbling of thunder.

Charlie was so heavy,
his bulging belly scraped
across the mountaintops,
causing great spears of lightning
to stab the hills and fields.

18

Charlie began to feel cold and lonesome.
From the corner of his eye,
a small drop of water squeezed out.
From the other eye,
another drop slipped out.
A storm of tears
gushed from Charlie's eyes.
The more he cried,
the smaller he shrank,
until there wasn't a single tear left,
and Charlie fell into a deep sleep.

For a while, all was quiet.

Suddenly, a voice rang out from below.
"Look at that beautiful little cloud!"

Charlie opened his eyes
and looked all around.
There were no other clouds in the sky.
All the people in the village,
the animals, the birds,
even the sun and mountains,
were smiling at him.

Charlie looked down at his reflection
in the water.
"Why is everyone smiling at me?"
he wondered.
"I'm not doing anything special.
I'm just being myself."

A soft voice from deep within Charlie answered,
"Being yourself
is the most special thing
you can ever be."